to Sue

THE ARCHITECTURAL TOURIST

SKETCH IMPRESSIONS OF EUROPE – FROM NORWAY TO NAPLES

Stuart.

Ian Stuart Campbell Hon FRIAS

for Sharon

ACKNOWLEDGEMENTS

The author is very grateful to the RIAS for the publication of this volume; to Robin McKechnie and the St Columba's Hospice for their agreement to the dedication and to the proceeds going to such an excellent cause; to Jon Jardine for the beauty and clarity of the design (as ever); to Sholto Humphries for the kind preface; Neil Baxter for his essay and editorial assistance and to Carol-Ann Hildersley for her work to turn round the production so effectively. On a personal note he is ever full of gratitude and love to his companion on these journeys and in life, Joyce and to his son Calum – who is following in the old man's architectural footsteps.

First Published 2012 by
The Royal Incorporation of Architects in Scotland, 15 Rutland Square, Edinburgh EH1 2BE

Content: Ian Stuart Campbell Hon FRIAS
Editor: Neil Baxter
Design: Jon Jardine (mail@jonjardine.com)

ISBN: 978-1-873190-67-8

A catalogue record of this book is available from the British Library.

All photos by Ian Stuart Campbell except photo of Ian Stuart Campbell by Sig. Emanuele Colomboni (San Costanzo) and photo of Sharon McCord by Wattie Cheung (her good friend).

CONTENTS

RIAS HEADQUARTERS, 15 RUTLAND SQUARE, EDINBURGH

The square was planned in 1819 by Archibald Elliot though most of its buildings, including no. 15, are by John Tait from the 1830s.

THE ARCHITECTURAL TOURIST

PRESIDENTIAL PREFACE

It is wholly appropriate that this book is dedicated to the late Sharon McCord. Sharon contributed a very great deal to the architectural profession and in support of the art of architecture – which she loved. It is typically generous of Stuart Campbell that he has insisted on all of the profits from this publication going to the St Columba's Hospice. The Royal Incorporation is delighted to publish this superb volume, to honour Sharon and to contribute to an extremely worthy cause.

In the summer of 2010 the second issue of the new *RIAS Quarterly* featured the first of what promised to be an occasional series of illustrated essays by Stuart Campbell. The topic, Rome, was thoroughly appropriate for a magazine published in July. Stuart's photographs displayed details, glimpses through windows, the corner of a courtyard and more expansive views down long vistas dappled with sunlight and shadow.

However it was Stuart's drawings which were the real delight. Stuart is a master of in-situ drawing, a technique promulgated by the Impressionists but a discipline which often proved too taxing, even for them. His drawings vary from the precision of the spare rendering of classical arcades in studied masterclasses in perspective, to looser exercises bringing statuary, low relief carving and buildings together in more rapidly sketched compositions, blurring the contrast between the manmade, artist's renderings of nature and the truly organic.

Stuart's written essays too are the impressions of an informed visitor. He arrives in his various destinations equipped with a highly developed eye for their cultural and architectural uniqueness. His essays, written and drawn, emphasise the special qualities of each of the European cities visited in this book.

Between that first outing in 2010 and the most recent *RIAS Quarterly*, featuring another extraordinary Italian city, Naples, Stuart has explored ten varied cities. In this, the first compendium of his drawings, photographs and essays, additional captions enlarge upon the minimal references which were included in their original publication. Together they become a quite unique and very special guide to the highlights of each city.

While this volume doesn't pretend to be like any standard guide book with maps and directions, there is little that is depicted here which is difficult to find if you choose to make these cities your destination. Each of Stuart's city visits has delivered a fascinating study. Together they testify to an extraordinary talent. The sum of their parts is, indeed, a very beautiful book.

Sholto

Sholto Humphries
President
The Royal Incorporation of Architects in Scotland

PLACA REIAL

Francesc Daniel Molina i Casamajó (mid 19th century)

A tranquil colonnaded oasis within the bustling city during daylight hours, Placa Reial transforms into a party place with clubs and restaurants each evening. The Lanterns still in use amid the palm trees were Antoni Gaudi's first design commission.

CITY VISIONS

THROUGH THE EYES OF IAN STUART CAMPBELL

The late Sharon McCord's enthusiastic encouragement of Stuart Campbell's proposal to bring an international flavour to the re-designed *RIAS Quarterly* testifies to her intelligence as an editor. Stuart's offer was a gift to any editor. Not only would his drawings emphasise the architectural highlights and quirky details which only an architect's or artist's eye might pick up, but Stuart is a keen observer who writes in an engaging style and whose camera lens superbly frames the defining moments and architectural glories of his many destinations.

Of course Stuart's productions in the *RIAS Quarterly*, just as in this compendium of his essays for what is now a well-established and highly regarded journal, are laid out on the pages in a manner which seems deceptively simple but testifies to the sympathetic eye of the third player in the endeavour, the, Berlin-based, Scots designer, Jon Jardine. Between them, Sharon, Stuart and Jon created a formula in that first essay on Rome which has been successfully repeated in nine subsequent pieces on Amsterdam, Barcelona, Berlin, Copenhagen, Florence, Naples, Norway (Bergen and Oslo) Paris and Valencia. Pen in hand, Stuart has taken up temporary residence in pavement cafés, commanding views of the roofscapes of Amsterdam and Paris, the boulevards of Barcelona and Berlin and city squares in Florence and Copenhagen.

Stuart's drawings of cities and buildings have two predominant modes. His renderings of the Duomo in Florence and Berlin's Galleries Lafayette, while depicting quite different buildings in sharply contrasting materials from quite different eras, share a degree of precision and architectural enquiry into the repeated rhythms of the classical embellishments of the former and the striated, largely frameless, glazing of the latter. In the squares of Rome and Copenhagen or La Rambla of Barcelona, his depictions are looser, more organic, perhaps reflecting more on the human activity which occurs around these buildings and within these landscapes. In his cityscapes of Amsterdam and Paris, variations in hatching describe the tonalities of different roof and wall surfaces and the intensity of light that plays upon them.

One further aspect of Stuart Campbell's drawings is that his medium is consistent, pen on paper. Yet these drawings are so lively, intricate, detailed, full of interest, nuance, light, shade, impression against precision, that their lack of colour becomes a virtue. Through Stuart's eye and his pen, the viewer is enabled to look. That is the great glory of this book. Through its pages its readership will revisit familiar places, seen in a new way, and be encouraged to revisit. And for those who have not yet experienced these cities, the majority of which Stuart reached via low cost airlines from Scottish airports, there are treats in store.

Mind you, one of Stuart Campbell's great heroes, the Italian landscape artist Giovanni Battista Lusieri, left a legacy of unrendered works. Ironically, this was not because he felt that the purity of his line might be compromised by colour, but because he put off colouring his images for a lifetime, storing them up for a time when the exquisite pleasure of rendering them in colour might be enjoyed to the full. Lusieri put off that pleasure for too long. Perhaps we should try Stuart out with a tin of top quality watercolour blocks. Who knows to what new visions that might lead?

Neil Baxter

AMSTERDAM

52.37°N, 4.89°E

PULITZER JETTY

Many adventurous Amsterdam hotels have their own jetty and some even offer cruises on their own canal boat. The Pulitzer's waterbus is a beautiful confection of oak, glass and brass which transports clients around the city and into a more elegant era.

UNIQUE PLACES EVOLVE SOMETIMES by reasons of architecture, geography, history, or people. Amsterdam is unique in so many ways, that it almost defies analysis. There are so many anomalies to consider that each visitor to the 'Dam will quickly build their own intimate understanding of this unique city and its 'horse shoe' grid plan.

From a 12th century village, Amsterdam became the world's richest city, trading in agriculture and diamonds, with the first ever Stock Exchange opening in 1602. The architecture reflected its prosperity in fine residences for merchants, financiers, craftsmen, doctors, lawyers, politicians and artists.

Lack of space along new canal quays forced houses to be built tall and narrow, characterised by high windows, decorative gables, steep internal stairs and a pulley outside to transport larger objects to upper floors. Often these residences also served as businesses with storage in attics and cellars.

Today Amsterdam manages to be at once, both lush and leafy (boasting more trees than Paris) yet with barely a patch of 'green' ground big enough to comfort a puppy. Tall, gently leaning trees line canals, growing miraculously in sand below hard paved walkways.

Sand is also the base beneath the distinctive herringbone paving, the bollards, the street furniture, and even the buildings. The jaunty angles, which readily appear, even on newly set bollards, and rakish reinforced gables, belie the fact that this urban fabric has resisted collapse for over 400 years. It appears as a complex dynamic balance where interlocking forces mutually support each other.

Logic and the parable of the two builders (Matthew 7) suggest that cities should not be constructed on sand. Certainly they should not be built 13 feet below sea level. Yet somehow Amsterdam has survived the Industrial Revolution, two World Wars, and vibration from cars, heavy lorries and rumbling trams. An ambitious underground Metro plan is however currently threatening this historic equilibrium. Thus far only excavations for the stations have progressed, but contract delays, vastly increased construction costs, and now settlement on some adjacent properties may jeopardise the project.

Civic determination to maintain 'quality of life' accolades for Amsterdam lies behind significant investment in other recent civic projects such as: ARTIS, Aquarium and Zoo buildings, new facilities at the Vondelpark, the Nemo Science and Tech Museum, the Van Gogh and Stedelijk museums, and the Rijksmuseum, the new music hall at Muziekgebouw and the huge new Central Library beside Centraal Station. All these bear witness to social priorities, which aim to improve the lives of all residents.

No cultural initiative, however, has had less impact on the built fabric and more effect on the appearance of the city than the Dutch adoption of bicycles. Basic upright 'grandpa bicycles', 'opafiets', are used by all ages, shapes, and genders. Heavy machines, with back pedal braking, are adapted with handlebar seats for children, or as a 'bakfiets', extended with a box for two more kids, livestock, or groceries.

Municipal support now provides that all parts of the city are accessible and safely linked by dedicated bike routes. Vigorously regulated 'Cyclist Priority' ensures caution from drivers of thrusting 4x4s, while each urgent 'ping' of a bicycle bell scatters pedestrians on all minor roads and junctions. Truly every cyclist has a "Golden Seat" – the ideal vantage from which to appreciate Amsterdam.

Old style street lamps (1883 on) have been replaced in some parts of Amsterdam, causing consternation among residents

Musiekgebouw Concert Hall for contemporary music by Danish architects 3XN (2005)

De Zuiderkerk, Hendrick de Keyser (1611), was the first Protestant Church in Amsterdam

View across docks from Library towards the ship shaped Science Centre, NEMO, Renzo Piano (1997)

The new Bibliotheek on 10 floors, Jo Coenen (2007), is now the largest public library in Europe

Lock Gates at Singel, the canal which was once the 'moat' around the medieval city

Cruise liners tie up alongside the Concert Hall, 3XN (2005)

Grass grows anywhere – even on a barge

Bright shutters keep out light

No lycra, no helmets – no brakes

Magna Plaza, CH Peters (1899) –characterful retail centre (1992) within former Post Office

Amsterdam School of the Arts, Teun Koolhaas (1996), a modern intervention across the road from the historic Rembrandt House Museum

RIJKSMUSEUM

Petrus J H Cuypers (1885)

The steep roofs of the Dutch neo-renaissance state museum are a distinctive landmark, visible across the entire city. 2013 celebrates ten years of reconstruction work to bring this Dutch national treasure back to the people.

HERENGRACHT

Herengracht, a popular 17th century residential area in which house widths were restricted.

REGULIERSGRACHT

Renowned for its uninterrupted views through nine bridges Regeliersgracht is a busy canal with tight angles to challenge long water buses.

CENTRUM SPUI

refurb.1996

A charming square formed in 1882 by filling in a canal dating from 1420. Recent renovation has made this a safe and attractive gathering place.

BERENSTRAAT

The centre of the city's 'boutique village' known as "de Negen Straatjes" or nine streets, Berenstraat links Prinzengracht and Kiesersgracht.

MAGNA PLAZA

C H Peters (originally built 1899)

Amsterdam's neo-gothic former post office was revitalised in 1992 as a multi level shopping centre on the model of Princes Square, Glasgow, with the intention of securing the building's survival for another century.

BARCELONA

41.38°N, 2.17°E

PORT VELL

View across marina towards Barceloneta.

EVERYONE LOVES BARCELONA. In design, architecture and planning, this city is first division. It presents its many historical layers with clarity. Roman and Gothic quarters; the innovative Cerda grid plan – which accommodated massive 19th century expansion; reinstated vernacular fisher-housing at Barceloneta; and reused Olympic residential communities are each well-defined and easily distinguished.

In spite of rich historical variety Barcelona is now renowned primarily for modern styling. Much of this reputation was achieved as part of the successful bid for the 1992 Olympics. According to David Mackay Hon FRIAS in his recent book *A Life in Cities* (RIAS Publishing 2009), informal discussion of architecture and planning was 'subversive' until Franco's death in 1975. The Olympic bid therefore released a torrent of pent-up progressive thinking and utopian enthusiasm from intellectuals and design professionals.

The resultant design energy and good taste still appears to inform more recent interventions within the city fabric. Astonishing metal and wire sculpture by Antoni Tapies grows courageously out of the roof above a traditional 19th century brick and iron building by Domenech I Montaner. It is not irreverent – yet it is hard to imagine listed building consent being granted in Scotland for anything quite so gutsy.

Across Passeig de Gracia from Gaudi's Pedrera a modern hotel presents metal sheet elevations reminiscent of horizontally slashed paper. The contextural incongruity of this is much of its charm. Further along Passeig de Gracia, "I'll de Discord" celebrates the diversity of four leading modernists including Gaudi (Casa Batllo).

Right at the city's heart, Avinguda de la Catedral offers useful pedestrian public space for markets and pageants while discreetly concealing underground parking out of sight below this historic sector. Yet even here, in what could have been a crusty ancient area, there are roof-top infinity pools and exciting colourful interventions as at the Santa Caterina Market. A spectacular undulating ceramic roof by Miralles and Tagliabue (EMBT) oversails original white painted walls dating from 1845 and brings new life to an old market hall. EMBT's architectural philosophy appears to disregard old and new and considers everything that has survived into the present as facing the same design challenge – to move forward.

Barcelona's most spectacularly decorated building dates from 1908 and was designed by Lluis Domenech I Montaner. Set in a narrow site within La Ribera, The Palau de la Musica Catalana is extraordinarily flamboyant even for the city of Gaudi. The richness of the external decoration is exceeded internally. Yet its underlying rational design has ensured this building remains a most successful concert venue. As a result it has had several major restoration and extension projects designed by Oscar Tusquets and Carlos Diaz.

In 1997 the building was declared a UNESCO world heritage site. Two years later further dramatic expansion occurred to create the Petit Palau – a state of the art, 538 seat, underground auditorium. Above, new red brick service towers enclose a new public space ideal for open-air performances and frame views of the original façade, now viewed through a modern full height glazed screen. It remains unique as a naturally lit concert hall.

Conservation in Barcelona appears to have found a happy balance which values the city's rich heritage without stifling progressive design and innovative architecture. Valiente y brillante!

Inspiring artworks along La Ramblas

Gaudi's chimneys on La Pedrera (1910) – inspiration for Star Wars?

Tiled roof at Santa Caterina Market, EMBT (2004) sweeps over the historic facades, forming a spacious flexible hall. Superficial similarities to the Scottish Parliament by the same practice exercise small minds

Former fishermens' Quarter now mostly leisure at Barceloneta

Audacious Torre Agbar, Jean Nouvel (2005)

High rise at the Olympic Port, Hotel Arts SOM and Torre Mapfre, Inigo Ortiz and Enrique León; Frank Gehry's fish sculpture (all 1992)

MACBA the museum of Contemporary Art , Richard Meier & Partners (1997)

Sculpted elevations at Sagrada Familia, Antoni Gaudi (started 1883)

Casa Batllo restored and revitalised by Gaudi (1906)

Palau de la Musica Catalana, Lluis Domenechi Montaner (1908), extension Oscar Tusquets and Carles Diaz (2004)

Petit Palau, Oscar Tusquets and Carles Diaz (2004)

La Pedrera, Antoni Gaudi (1910)

BORN
Tall narrow lanes of the Born.

TORRE D'ALTA MAR

Carles Buígas, Ramon Road and Joseph M Roda (1931)

The audacious cable car connecting the beach to Montjuic hillside was originally intended to serve Barcelona's 1929 exhibition but was two years too long in construction. The tower now houses a restaurant and viewing gallery, as well as the cable car station.

LA RAMBLA

Unusual 1.2km long retail street with central pedestrian route for kiosks and seating, flanked by busy single carriageways on each side. An exciting promenade with loads of vitality. The restaurants who skillfully serve across the traffic from pavement shops may disagree that this is a brilliant urban solution.

PLACA DE LA SEU

This reconstructed forecourt to the Cathedral is well suited to events and open air markets while conveniently concealing parking below ground.

PALAU DE LA MÚSICA CATALANA

Lluís Domènech i Montaner (1908)

Above the main entrance the original rich elevation is an architectural marvel.

LA PEDRERA

Antoni Gaudi (1912)

Gorgeous curvaceous stone and wrought iron almost begs for some blown glass to complete the organic appearance but, as in nature, close inspection reveals a logical structure, designed to allow column free internal space. Nothing is random.

BERGEN

60.38°N, 5.34°E

OSLO

59.95°N, 10.76°E

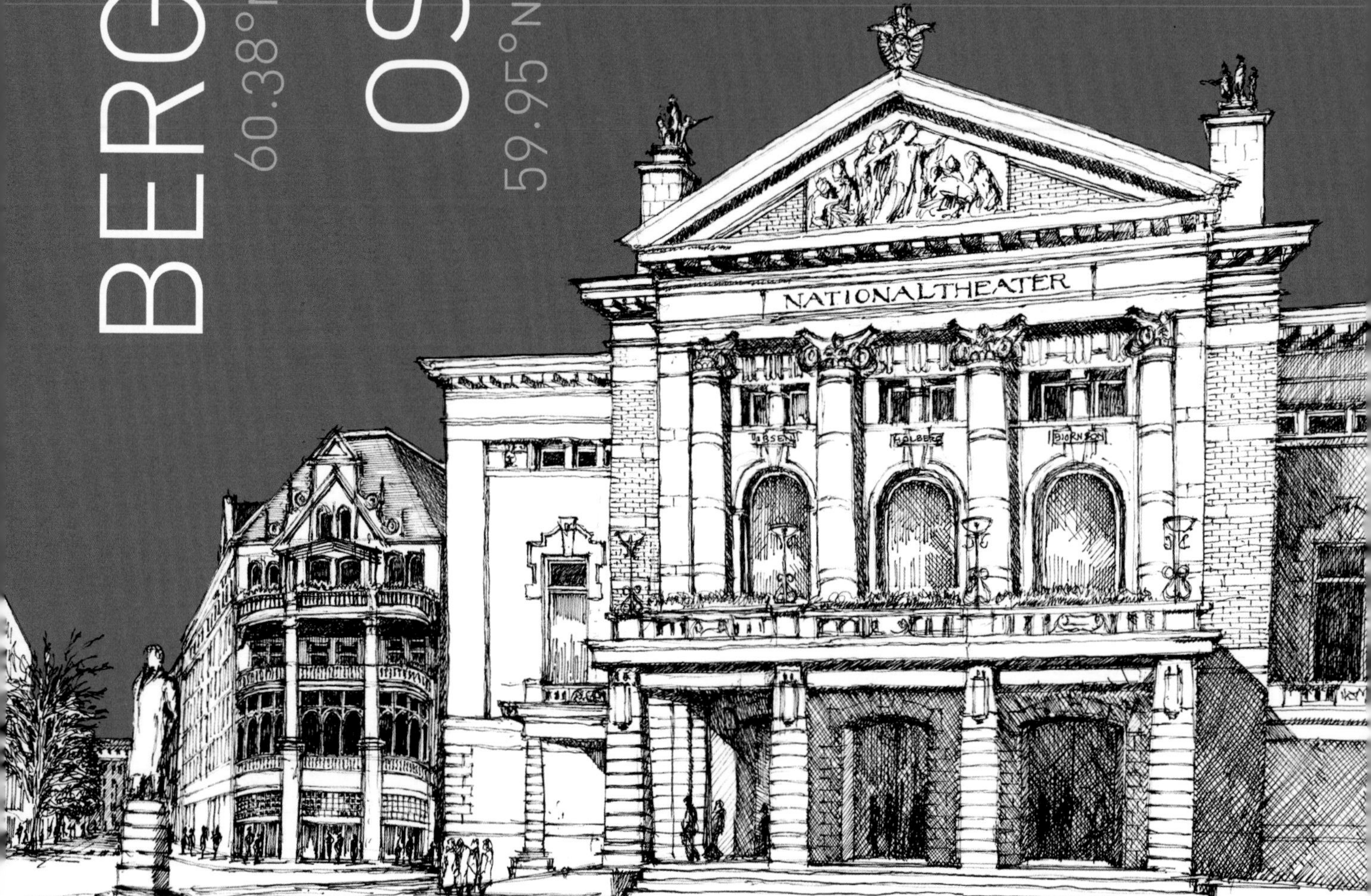

NATIONALTHEATRET, OSLO

Henrik Bull (1899)

The National Theatre (Nationaltheatret) is considered to be the cultural home of Ibsen. Adjacent is Theatercaféen (1900) renovated in 1971 back to its original Art Nouveau style, under architect Hans Gabriel Finne, and now found on the New York Times list of the world's best, Vienna-styled, cafes.

SO MUCH SEEMS FAMILIAR. The landscape, conifers, traffic cones, even the weather could be Scotland. A population slightly under five million is almost parallel too. Yet the atmosphere is distinctively Scandinavian. Trolls and Vikings take the place of kilted tat in gift shops and a strong NOK - Norwegian Kroner – means even a coffee is an expensive purchase.

A cynic would observe that July is a very Scottish month for Oslo to close all city railways. Yet major infrastructure contractors only get a short work window in a Scandinavian climate. Summer is thus boom time for maintenance, tunnelling and construction.

An impressive tunnel network takes heavy road and rail traffic through Oslo without obvious disruption. Tunnels too make it possible for the spectacular Bergen-Oslo rail-line to climb to 4000ft (1222m) where mountain tops and glaciers are easily accessible. There is no guilt here. No fenced off compound restricting public access to precious high places - as at Cairngorm.

Norwegians are positively encouraged to bike, hike, ski or simply take the mountain air. In 1957 their government consolidated the right to roam over open land. The Friluftsliv movement (translated as "open air living") further established outdoor recreation as part of the nation's culture. This includes hyttes - holiday retreats which originally were very basic timber cabins but now typically offer many more comforts. Originally self built, families often own at least one hytte for weekends while good employers retain waterfront and mountain hyttes for staff recreation. Again there is no 'holiday home' guilt.

Oslo's vision for 2020 anticipates a population increase from 250,000 to 310,000. Stylish flats, retail and offices leading towards a dramatic new Art Centre by Renzo Piano are transforming redundant boat-yards at Aker Brygge. In fine weather this already offers a convincing Mediterranean waterfront. An even more audacious commercial development, 'Barcode', is now under construction behind Snohetta's iconic Opera House. This promises an exciting cultural sector with dedicated galleries for Munch and a 21st century public library.

Conspicuous prosperity is all around. Gender equality is high in workplaces. Large companies have now achieved 40% female participation on boards. Unemployment is low. Happiness and personal satisfaction are high. The Legatum Prosperity Index placed Norway at no.1 in the world. The *New York Times* attributed Norwegian financial success to "working women". Apparently Norway combines the world's highest female employment rates with an impressively high birth rate and extensive maternity - and paternity - provision. A successful outcome for such a small country. Especially for one that recently celebrated a whole century of independence from its larger, stronger, more powerful neighbour.

Norway's independent government apparently does not seek re-election on promises of reducing taxation, but instead supports family initiatives and caps costs of child-care with subsidies. It also still finds funds (€500m) for a spectacular Opera House, art galleries, public libraries, hospitals, and impressive infrastructure and transport. Norway represents one of the world's last fully functioning welfare states, yet economic indicators remain positive. No need for austerity – or guilt – here.

The *New York Times*' financial appraisal did however also mention that Norway has oil. And when you've got oil, the possibilities are endless!

BARCODE, OSLO

Competition promoter: OSU a consortium comprising Government Property, a private developer, and Norwegian State Railways (completion 2014)

Oslo authorities approved the controversial "Barcode" high rise development plan in 2003 in the face of considerable local opposition. An International Design competition won by Dark Architects (Oslo), A-Lab and MVRDV (Rotterdam), proposed a new public space between the station and the new Opera House and a series of individual bespoke towers along the waterfront, each with wide gaps to allow air, light and views.

OSLO OPERA HOUSE

Snohetta (2008)

Oslo's angular new Opera House rises out of the water like an iceberg. Public access across the sloping roofs gives unique views over the city and fjord. Warm timber slatted surfaces curve around within the vast foyer and contrast with the colder white marble and glass exteriors.

Aker Brygge commercial redevelopment of former boatyards, Oslo, Telje-Torp-Aasen Arkitektkontor AS (1986)

City Hall, Oslo, Arnstein Arneberg and Magnus Poulsson (1950)

Karl Johans gate, Oslo's main street connects Central Station to the Royal Palace

Oslo Opera House, Snohetta Architects (2008), with Barcode Development behind

Musicians and street performers gather at the high point on Karl Johans Gate, where a distant view of the Palace draws tourists up the long precessional avenue

AKERSHUS FESTNING

Akershus Festning, a fortress since 1290, has a commanding site overlooking Oslo's busy harbour and fjord. Visiting cruise liners regularly cast long shadows over the still large fleet of tall masted sailing vessels which contribute a romantic Nordic character to the city's waterfront.

Colourful timber housing at Bryggen, Bergen

Colour enriches Vagsallmenningen square, Bergen (c. 1700)

A high level lochan separates Finse station from the glacier

Rail halt at Finse 1,222 metres (4,000 ft) above sea level. Passengers are encouraged to disembark and take the mountain air

Pedestrianised Marken, Bergen

Norwegian mountain landscape with remote 'hytte' for family recreation

Larger vessels dock at Strandsiden, across the inlet from Bryggen

BRYGGEN, BERGEN

Founded around 1070, some remaining buildings from c.1700; World Heritage Status 1979

The colourful timber gables of Bryggen is the popular image of Norway. The narrow gaps between lead to a timber wonderland of impossible cantilevers and improbable stairways, forming small dwellings and workshops, now mostly restaurants. Although subject to many fires through the centuries some buildings on the site date from 1700 and reflect Bergen's origins.

BRANDENBURG GATE

Carl Gotthard Llanghans (1778)

Designed as a symbol of peace, the building became identified with the Nazis. Extensive restoration was required after severe war damage. However the Gate's proximity to the Berlin Wall meant that these restoration works were delayed until 2002, after the reunification of east and west Germany.

BERLIN 52.52°N, 13.41°E

FEW CITIES CAN BOAST buildings by Norman Foster, Richard Rogers, Helmut Jahn, Renzo Piano, Hans Hollien, James Stirling, Rem Koolhaas, Frank Gehry, I.M.Pei, Jean Nouvel, Peter Eisenman, MBM, Daniel Libeskind, David Chipperfield, OMA, 3XN and more. Yet a short afternoon stroll around Berlin can take in works by all of them. More forethought could include further greats from previous generations such as Le Corbusier, Mies van der Rohe and Schinkel.

This architectural showcase is a result of very particular circumstances. War followed by peacetime partition led Berlin to very dark times. The German Democratic Republic (GDR) constructed the Berlin Wall (August 1961) initially as a barbed wire fence isolating West Berlin. It became the wide clearing "death strip" extending 96 miles.

A building program by International Building Exhibition (IBA) began to develop gap sites caused by the Wall within West Berlin (1987). IBA intended to encourage local architects, diversity and careful urban redevelopment. Architects from 15 countries responded to invitational design competitions. Once the wall was removed in 1989, regeneration created plentiful opportunities for this international architects' Who's Who. Many were already in Berlin and keen to design prestigious government, diplomatic and commercial commissions.

Masterplans were prepared for derelict areas such as Potsdamer Platz. Pre-war this had been Europe's busiest centre. It became the world's biggest building site. Daimler-Benz appointed Renzo Piano to build their 20 storey offices and to oversee 19 other adjacent buildings, while Hans Kollhoff designed his 25 storey centrepiece, Kolhoff Tower.

Helmut Jahn challenged the masterplan further with his 26 storey curved glass tower with an elliptical public space beneath a tented roof – the Sony Centre. It also incorporates surviving parts of the Hotel Esplanade, as featured in 'Cabaret`. The building had to be moved in one piece over 75 metres and is now preserved behind dramatic sheer glass curtain walling.

Potsdamer Platz set standards for public realm which are now the envy of UK authorities. Materials and landscaping defines pedestrian, cycle and vehicle zones, while comprehensive underground parking integrates sensibly with underground railway stations, offices and retail. Informal seating is abundant beneath decorative trees and canopies which mitigate effects of adjacent tall buildings.

Spectacular new retail centres along Friedrichstrasse link seamlessly below ground while presenting varied architecture to street level. Jean Nouvel's 'Lafayette' reflects the Parisian store. Its curved glass frontage is recognisable as a background to recent trendy car advertisements.

Extensive work has also restored surviving buildings throughout the city. Evidence remains in bullet holes that some of the fiercest war episodes occurred in Berlin. Facades show scars and holes which now contrast eerily with modern elevations.

The history of Berlin is long and complex. In 1991 the Bundestag voted to move the West German administration back from Bonn and Berlin regained capital status.

Once more Berlin is a colourful, artistic and cultural centre where opinions are freely voiced - often against architects, planners and designers. Berlin presents a surprisingly rich, comprehensible and rewarding architectural narrative to enjoy and discuss. Just don't expect consensus.

JEWISH MUSEUM

Daniel Libeskind (2001)

The design has an intentionally disorientating plan and elevation treatment which, combined with sloping floor levels, ensures a thought provoking and even disturbing experience.

GALERIES LAFAYETTE

Jean Nouvel (1996)

Parisian style brought to Berlin with a crisp glass facade matched by the glittering inverted glazed cone forming a welcome atrium within this huge department store. The basement level links to a retail mall running the full length of Friedrichstrasse, sensibly connecting the series of modern architectural retail blocks.

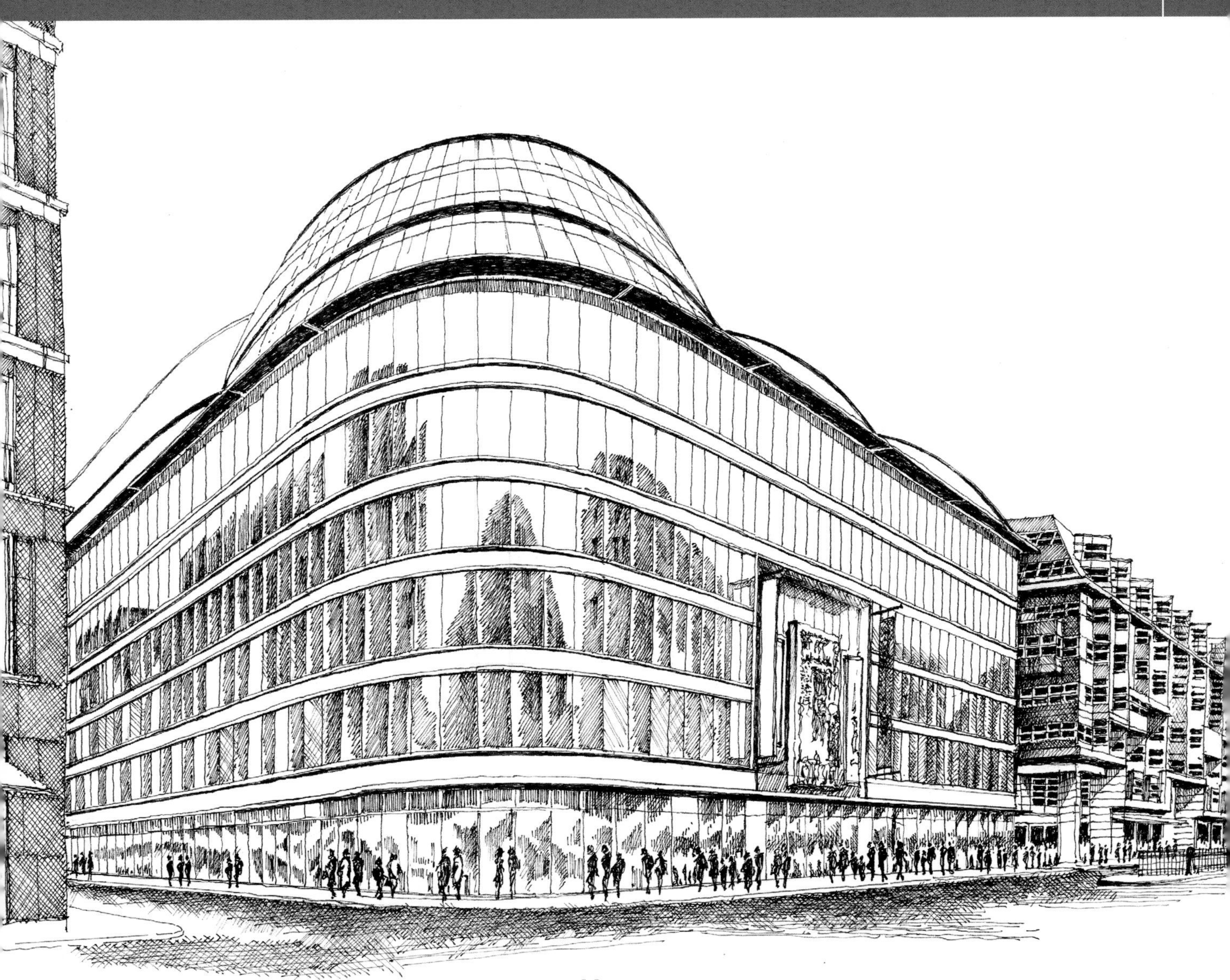

Trabant (manufactured by VEB Sachsenring – 1957-91)

'Marie Elisabeth Luders Haus' Parliamentary Library at Reichstag, Stephan Braunfels Architect (2003)

Covered atrium at Sony Centre, Helmut Jahn (2000)

TV Tower, Herman Henselmann (1969)

Memorial to the Murdered Jews of Europe, Peter Eisenman (2004)

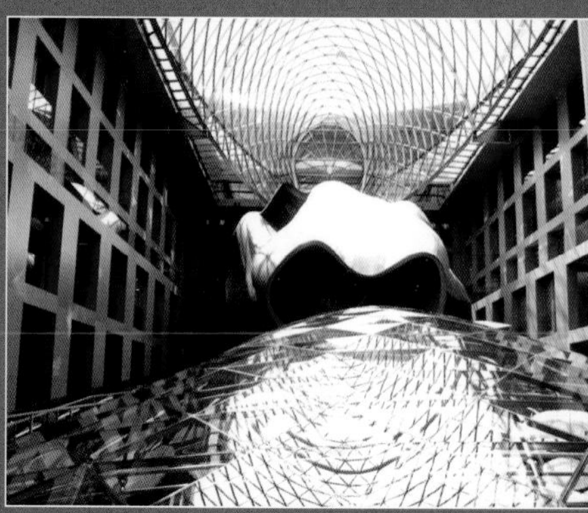

Sculptural glazed atrium within mixed-use building including residential, conference and DZ Bank at Pariser Platz, Frank O Gehry (2000)

DB Building towering above the Sony Centre, Helmut Jahn (2000)

Rebuilt Friedrichstrasse at "Checkpoint Charlie". Triangle Building, Kleihues + Kleihues (1996)

Residential sector of Daimler-Chrysler Quarter, Richard Rogers Partnership (1999)

Reichstag, Paul Wallot (1894), reconstructed to a design by Sir Norman Foster (1999)

Tensile roof over the Sony Centre, Helmut Jahn (2000)

Intelligently integrated urban transport, low level rail station and car parking beneath Potsdamer Platz, BPA (2006)

POTSDAMER PLATZ

Masterplan by Hilmer and Sattler (completed 2009)

Built on vacant land left after the removal of the Berlin Wall. Renzo Piano's Daimler complex culminating in a 20 storey tower (left above), Hans Kolhoff's 25 storey tower (centre), and the Sony Centre Bahn Tower (right) by Helmut Jahn provide exemplars of successful public realm design with busy and accessible commercial ground floor uses and commendable integrated transport and parking.

MARSCHALL BRUCKE

The bridge carrying Wilhelmstrasse across the Spree once marked the border between east and west Germany. The modern bright architecture reconstructed along the river frontage at Reichstagufer remains a "white crosses memorial" site with an art installation remembering those who died trying to escape across no man's land to West Berlin.

FERNSEHTURM

Fritz Dieter, Gunter Frankenstein, and Werner Ahrendt (1969)

Designed as a statement of the GDR's importance, the tower, with its space satellite topping, is still visible throughout the re-unified city, and now provides an impressive public viewing gallery and a rotating restaurant.

PAZZI CHAPEL, SANTA CROCE

attributed to Filippo Brunelleschi (1443)

It is inevitable that buildings still in service five centuries after their construction will only release their secrets slowly. The Pazzi Chapel, adjoined to the Cloisters at Basilica di Santa Croce, has various dates, depending on the chosen source. All agree however that this is a masterpiece of renaissance architecture.

FIRENZE

43.77°N, 11.25°E

FLORENCE HAS IMMENSE RICHES in sculpture, art and architecture. Yet not everything is quite as it first appears.

Consider Michelangelo's David. On completion (1504) the sculptor and his supporters campaigned strongly for a prominent site at the entrance to the Palazzo Vecchio as the huge weight precluded it from being lifted onto the Duomo. Leonardo da Vinci – reportedly unimpressed by Michelangelo's work – preferred a less imposing location under cover in the adjacent loggia. Had Leonardo prevailed it might never have been necessary to remove the original into the Accademia Gallery for protection in 1873. A replica was substituted in 1910. It is convincing - but not authentic.

Likewise Ghiberti's doors at Florence's 12th century Baptistry were removed to the Museo dell'Opera del Duomo in 1990. The gilt bronze panels were so admired by Michelangelo that he named them the 'Gates of Paradise'. Centuries later these originals were removed to be laser cleaned. Again reproduction panels are now substituted. Convincing - but not authentic.

Arriving at the understated San Lorenzo church a visitor might easily be distracted by the vibrant adjacent market. To miss its spectacular interior and sacristies, one by Michelangelo and an older one by Brunelleschi, would be folly. Brunelleschi's rebuilding of this church waited a century for Michelangelo's marble façades, but 16th century austerity left this masterpiece eternally 'undressed'.

The vast Santa Croce fared better with its ornate frontage, yet an adjacent cloister leads to an unmarked gem. The Pazzi Chapel, thought to be among Brunelleschi's finest work, was completed (1443) only three years before his death.

Florence Cathedral, designed by Arnolfo di Cambio (1294), took 120 years to construct before Brunelleschi won the competition (1419) resolving the structural challenge of the impossibly huge dome using ingenious stone chains as 'ring beams'. Surprisingly the Duomo also remained 'undressed' until the 1880s when white, green and red marble was applied (designer: Emilio de Fabris).

Consider also the historic bridges across the Arno, demolished (1944) by retreating German forces. Original stones and statues were used to faithfully reinstate the damage. Convincing – but not authentic.

Thankfully the Ponte Vecchio was spared destruction, supposedly on the Fuhrer's personal instruction. As sole authentic survivor it reveals so much more about life since 1345 than any replica. The bridge originally accommodated fishmongers, butchers and tanners on stall tables. The projecting back-shops and upper floors were later additions, when goldsmiths became favoured as more fragrant traders on the bridge.

An audacious project for Cosimo I de Medici transformed the Ponte Vecchio (1565). A covered link of around one kilometre was built between the Palazzo Vecchio and the new Palazzo Pitti. It passed through the Uffizi Gallery; formed a tall arcade along the river; crossed the Ponte Vecchio [forming a fourth floor]; passed round Torre dei Mannelli on massive brackets; through the church of Santa Felicita and over houses in Oltrarno. Vasari's Corridor truly demonstrates the architecture of absolute power.

Florence's renowned Niccollo Macchiavelli become inextricably associated with duplicity. His keen interest in conspiracy and the legitimacy – or otherwise – of authority earned him imprisonment and torture in 1513. Perhaps we should simply enjoy Florence's vast treasure and not be too concerned with the niceties of what's 'real' - or what, for the best of reasons, simply pretends.

PONTE VECCHIO

Taddeo Gaddi (rebuilding attributed to Neri di Fioravanti, 1345); upper corridor Giorgio Vasari (1565)

Bridges were long sited at this narrowest point on the Arno but a number of timber predecessors were swept away in floods leading ultimately to the introduction of stone construction in 1345 which permitted the later additions of multi-level accommodation which gives this bridge such distinction.

SKETCH ELEVATION VIEWED ACROSS ROOFTOPS

The Campanile was started in 1334, to a design by the 67 year old painter Giotto di Bondone and was completed by Francesco Talenti in 1359 with Giotto's intended spire replaced by a projecting public viewing gallery. The Duomo (Basilica de Santa Maria del Fiore) commenced in 1296 to the design of Arnolfo di Cambio and was completed in 1436, once Filippo Brunelleschi's ring beam idea made support for the vast dome possible. The decorative marble facade appears to have had a more vexatious history with several false starts until achieving its present, almost complete, appearance in 1887. The drum gallery around the base of the dome remains uncovered and, over the centuries, has been the source of much controversy.

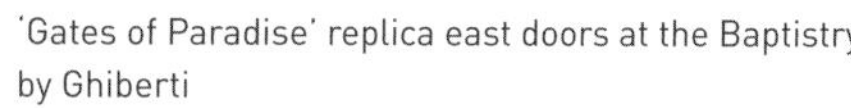

'Gates of Paradise' replica east doors at the Baptistry, by Ghiberti

Soft Florentine pantiled roofscape peppered with masts and dishes

Iconic view across the Arno to Florence from Piazzale Michelangelo

Abundance of ancient sculpture within Loggia dei Lanzi (1382), Simone di Francesco Talenti (1382)

Glimpse of Florentine opulence

Successful modern intervention at Via dei Castellani

Duomo with dome ring beam still unclad

Among Florence's oldest buildings the octagonal Baptistry (1128)

Basilica di San Lorenzo, Filippo Brunelleschi (1459), remarkable church still awaiting its marble cladding

Ponte Vecchio

The Vasari Corridor snakes its route around and across the historic city

PIAZZA DEL DUOMO

Baptistry (1059-1128)

The octagonal baptistry is one the oldest buildings in Florence's yet was used to baptise all catholics in the city until the end of the 19th century.

PIAZZA DELLA SIGNORIA

Equestrian Statue Duke Cosimo I

Giambologna (1595)

Now widely used for public events, music or modern dance this was the site of Savonarola's "Bonfire of the Vanities" and ultimately his own death in 1498, when he was burnt at the stake for heresy.

PONTE VECCHIO, VASARI CORRIDOR

Giorgio Vasari (1565)

The open area under the corridor at the centre of the bridge attracts unlicensed traders displaying their goods on sheets. Grabbing the four corners of the sheets lets them quickly relocate in a never ending game of "cat and mouse" with the police.

LOGGIA DEI LANZI

Simone di Francesco Talenti (1382)

This unique open air gallery, adjoining the Uffici, shelters a collection of antique and renaissance sculptures and is guarded by two Medici Lions - one dating from 1598 the other from 200BC.

KØBENHAVN

55.67°N, 12.57°E

CHRISTIANSBORG PALACE

Thorvald Jorgensen (commenced 1740, completed 1928)

As home to the Prime Minister's Office, the Supreme Court and the Parliament, access to the Royal Palace across the Marble Bridge was restored and upgraded in 1996 in time for the city's year as European Capital of Culture.

BEFORE THE SEATTLE BEAN companies moved onto each UK street corner, the smell of real coffee was a rare treat. One small pavilion in Glasgow's trendy West End provided this aroma, in a heady 1960's combo with food, Scandinavian products, and artworks. Here was my early introduction to Danish design, and to the 'grooks' of Piet Hein, (1906-1996) a Danish polymath, designer, philosopher and writer, who I now know produced in excess of 7,000 of these pithy aphorisms.

"There is one art, no more, no less;
to do all things, with artless-ness"

Hein's grook concisely presages the 'no frills' approach now universally identified with Danish design. Clean, simple, uncluttered lines distinguish Danish products: cutlery, furniture, bicycle frames, even thin 'flat screen' traffic lights, and of course, buildings. There appears to be a real public interest in design. Annual architecture open days in May, stylish retail displays, a prestigious riverside 'architecture exhibition centre', and a centrally located Danish Design Centre (DDC) beside Tivoli Gardens and the City Hall Square, ensure that even taxi drivers seem well informed and able to talk about design.

The three level Danish Design Centre leads by example. Clear and simple analysis of design projects ranging through health care innovations, toys, and iconic chair design, de-mystifies the process. On entry, just beyond the shop, a ten-point guide to assessment of "good" building design is unequivocal and easy to use. Characteristics for good value building design in the 21st century are noted as: intuitive, innovative, functional, honest, responsible, shaped and styled, user oriented, aesthetic, durable, and good business.

Most would agree with this checklist, but it is also interesting to consider one notable omission: 'context'. The Danish Design Centre approach promotes a more clinical assessment for each new building as an entity. This would appear to avoid emotional and sentimental confusion around 'context', which so often frustrates and de-rails serious design discussions in the UK. It also allows a more contemporary architectural response within each setting. Consequently, throughout the city there are vigorous glass and steel infill projects, abutting half-timbered and historic frame constructions.

Iconic new cultural buildings also proclaim their contemporary identity. The new Royal Library addition (Schmidt Hammer Lassen Architects) is a striking, angular, polished granite building, now known as 'the Black Diamond'. It massively extends the gentle 1906 original library, built in gardens behind the Parliament building, and creates another new significant landmark on the waterfront. The Opera (Henning Larsen Architects) is the most visible building in the inner harbour due to its prominent site. The tall glazed foyers and generous forecourt look out across the water and are protected below an enormous cantilevered roof canopy. There is now a dynamic architectural and visual balance here as the new Playhouse of the Royal Theatre (Lundgaard & Tranberg Arkitekter) reaches out from the opposite bank. The vast bulk of this theatre nestling between the rococo Frederiksstaden and the busy, picturesque, and colourful 17th century Nyhavn quayside, originally caused controversy but now seems to be respected, even by the well-informed taxi drivers.

Copenhagen's maritime roots remain extremely strong. The city centre occupies several islands and successfully presents itself as a series of spacious canals and waterfronts. Even ambitious new master-plans commence by sub-dividing huge 200 hectare sites, using extensions to existing waterways in order to create manageable development sites. Major new projects are currently proposed at Nordhavn by architects COBE/SLETH, and even more ambitious and already under construction is the New Orestad City, slowly emerging out of open space near the airport, following masterplans by Studio Daniel Libeskind and KHR Arkitekter. Already new concepts in urban and suburban living are taking shape and setting new standards which will doubtless be emulated elsewhere.

Copenhagen has managed its growth over recent centuries (population now 1.7m) by embracing the best and most innovative contemporary design and town planning. Classicism, romanticism and 17th century mercantile buildings co-exist in unusual comfort with 'functional modernism', honed and evolved by Arne Jacobsen, Vilhelm Lauritzen and others throughout the 20th century. The Danish architectural press has coined a nice phrase, and without reference to a 'grook', looks forward to Copenhagen's role developing as an "Architectural Exploratorium for the new Millennium."

NYHAVN WATERFRONT AND PLAYHOUSE LOOKING ACROSS TO 'OPEREAN'

On the quayside is the well mannered Royal Danish Playhouse, Lundgaard & Tranberg Arkitekter (2007) which opens onto a wide timber walkway, a popular place to people watch in the sunny weather. Assuming Opera-goers in Copenhagen arrive by boat, the impressively long cantilevered roof structure offers some high level shelter for those entering the huge, bulbous glazed foyer, Henning Larsen Architects (2004).

PISTOLSTRAEDE

An authentic lane off busy Ostergade, which bristles with colourful small shops, cafes and activity operating out of tiny vernacular buildings.

KONGENS NYTORV

Copenhagen's main public square was laid out by King Christian V (in 1670) who is celebrated in the central equestrian statue. This somewhat formal planted garden contrasts with the adjacent, revitalised, Nyhavn quayside, now a colourful and trendy meeting place.

Sunny north quay at Nyhavn

Popular meeting place, Nyhavn

Pleasure craft sail from Nyhavn

Vertical garden planted at the European Environment Agency in Kongens Nytorv

Historic vessels line the canal at Nyhavn

NYHAVN WATERFRONT

The short canal basin designed for cargo and fishing boats (1673) is now home to picturesque sailing vessels. Colourful timber and stucco townhouses along the north quay face larger mansions and commercial offices across the water.

AMAGERTORV / STROGET

Jan Gehl (1962)

Described as the longest pedestrian shopping area in Europe and renowned as an early example of pedestrianisation, Stroget will always appeal. The Stork Fountain (1894) at Amagertorv helps to define an irregular shaped open space surrounded by eclectic buildings, some dating from 1600.

The 'Black Diamond' extension to historic Royal Danish Library, Schmidt Hammer Lassen Architects (1999)

Royal Danish Playhouse, Lundgaard & Tranberg Arkitekter (2007)

New Playhouse meets the old town

National Bank of Denmark by Arne Jacobsen (1971)

Stylish waterfront apartments Strandgade, Christianshavn (2008)

'Operaen' Opera House, Henning Larsen Architects (2004)

NAPOLI

40.83°N, 14.25°W

VOMERO HILLTOP

Castel Saint'Elmo (1325) reconfigured by Pedro Luis Escriva (1537) and below it the San Martino Monastic complex (14th century) have visually dominated the Vomero hill behind Naples since the 14th century.

FAMILIARITY CAN DISAPPOINT. Branded retail outlets show little regional sensitivity, instead favouring standardisation. Identical buildings offer comforting familiarity, but do they breed satisfaction or contempt?

Savvy 19th century visitors to Naples surely found the architectural 'déjà vu' of the place stimulating. The city's major square, Piazza del Plebiscito, seems immediately familiar. The flanking colonnades (Leopoldo Laperuta 1809) evoke St Peter's Square, yet confusingly the centrepiece (Basilica de San Francesco de Paola (1817-46) by Pietro Bianchi) is based on another Roman icon - the Pantheon.

Nearby the sheer exuberance of Galleria Umberto I overcomes any surprise at finding Milan's magnificent Galleria Vittorio Emanuele II (1868) cloned in Naples - thirty years later. Just as in Milan glazed arcades meet beneath a vast dome, with rich detailing and exuberant mosaic patterns. In Milan they link Piazza del Duomo to Piazza della Scala. The cruciform plan however seems less comfortable on the sloping site in Naples where three of four entrances require steps. The main access opens from the west - Via Toledo - with the secondary south entrance obliquely facing Teatro di San Carlo, behind an elaborate colonnaded crescent. This facade somewhat overwhelms its historic neighbour which has enjoyed continuous service as a theatre since 1737.

The sheer abundance of antiquity in Naples ensures familiarity which, while not necessarily inducing contempt, has encouraged irreverent re-workings. Castel Nouvo (1280) displays numerous audacious architectural interventions, including five gigantic towers (1450) and later the white frilly 'triumphal arch', jammed between two of these sombre silos. This flamboyance is credited to Milanese architect Pietro di Martino with Catalan artists invited by Alfonso d'Aragona whose conquest of the city is celebrated in the renaissance panels.

Castel Sant'Elmo has dominated the Naples skyline since 1275, initially as a residential palace but later significantly reconfigured by Valencian military architect Pedro Luis Escriva (1537). Escriva introduced the innovative hexagonal star perimeter to form an impenetrable 'stronghold'- possibly the inspiration for Robert Adam's Fort George. Sant'Elmo became a jail for political prisoners in 1604 and a military prison until 1952. Recent restoration revealed generations of incongruous interventions but also introduced lifts, an auditorium and a library, allowing the building to join the Naples Museum Circuit in 1982. Sharing Vomero Hill is the beautiful San Martino monastic complex (1325) also intended to be impenetrable - but in a different way. Both buildings now offer public access and present sumptuous cultural treasures.

Castel dell'Ovo stands on the tiny outcrop of Megaris which, around three thousand years ago, was part of the Greek settlement of Parthenope, later Neapolis. From this foundation Naples became one of the oldest continuously occupied cities in Europe. In the first century BC a Roman Patrician built his residential Castel here, which, fortified six centuries later, became a monastery (492 AD) before being rebuilt as a fortification [11th century] and restructured to its present form during the Spanish Viceroyalty (1504 – 1713).

Over the centuries Naples' strategic location has exposed the city to invasions from Greeks, Spanish, French, Saracens and even the Roman Empire. The city also survived commercial invasions such as the 18th century 'volcano tourism' illustrated in the super Scottish National Gallery 2012 exhibition of the work of Giovanni Battista Lusieri, "Expanding Horizons". The current, potentially damaging, swell in 'cruise liner tourism' is a form of relatively benign contemporary invasion which may, in time, rejuvenate Neapolitan tourism and encourage lengthier stays in this unusually familiar, unique, city.

View across the Bay of Naples towards Vesuvius

Thriving sea port impacts on central Naples

High density housing climbs the historic Parthenope hill

Gigantic vessels now bring thousands of day tourists to Naples

A delightful Neapolitan dome tops the baroque Chiesa di Santa Maria in Portico, Nicola Longo (1632)

Neapolitan wedding photo shoot – no trees required

Rococo Cloister at Santa Chiara with unusual flamboyant majolica tiling, Domenico Antonio Vaccaro (1742)

Welcome colour in a challenging environment

Flight of stairs entering Galleria Umberto I, Emanuele Rocco (1891)

GALLERIA UMBERTO I

Emanuele Rocco (1891)

A stunning full size replica of Milan's Galleria. A slightly less exclusive retail offer but still presenting a stylish image.

SANTA CHIARA

Cloisters by Domenico Antonio Vaccaro (1742)

A tranquil cloistered church courtyard in the centre of Naples, extensively decorated with colourful majolica tiling to columns and benches.

VIA CHAIAI

Classical Greek influences remain in the Parthenope sector of the City.

CASTEL DELL'OVO

The oldest fortification in Naples (c. 1140) would present a challenge to assailants as it rises vertically out of the sea on all sides.

CASTEL NOUVO

Numerous incongruous architectural interventions define the story of this fortress but none clearer than the frilly entrance section (c. 1279), inserted between the sturdy stone towers.

48.87°N, 2.35°E

PARIS

LA GRANDE ARCHE

Johann Ottoman Von Spreckelsen, works completed by Paul Andreu (1989)

Paris's purpose built business district, La Defense, now presents a dynamic high rise skyline at the western end of the extended Champs Élysées. The gigantic Grande Arche, promoted by President Francois Mitterand and designed to celebrate humanitarian ideals, rather than military success, now architecturally trumps the Arc de Triomphe.

CHEFS OCCASIONALLY DE-CONSTRUCT attractive recipes and learn or adapt from successful techniques of others. On a grander scale architects similarly enjoy de-layering cities and their complex urban history, in a similar spirit of enquiry and pursuit of comprehension. Organic medieval city layouts after all, reveal much about the lives and priorities of previous generations.

Paris before Napoleon III became Emperor in 1852 probably looked like many other huge expanding European cities. The centre reportedly suffered from high population density and the concomitant hygiene problems. Public authority may also have been an issue, as several regimes had already been overthrown in the first half of that century. The new Paris, generally credited to Baron Haussmann but undoubtedly also supported by the Emperor, renovated the centre. It emerged with little of the old city for students and historians to analyse.

This huge transformation must surely have been accomplished via one of the largest ever, compulsory purchase initiatives. It must have been reassuring, if not actually essential, to have the support of a new reforming Emperor, on a venture of this scale.

Regulations were adapted to define street widths and building appearance. Building lines, eaves heights and storey alignment had to be regular and even roof pitches were required to be set at 45 degrees. Generous boulevards, up to 30m wide and high quality stone frontages, were created and now distinguish the Haussmann period of renovation in Paris. Together the whole confection gives an impression in places that the city centre is one large palace. Scale is enormous. Distances seem huge, open spaces appear vast and where five or six boulevards come together, the junctions defy perspective in their width, breadth and unmarked complexity.

A further, if not quite equally dramatic, 'French revolution' occurred again during the presidency of Francois Mitterand during the 1980's. His aim, to give Paris a new modern grandeur, created another distinctive new skyline, three miles to the west of the historical axis connecting the Louvre and The Arc de Triomphe. This plan extended the Champs Elysees, forming a visual as well as a physical link between the new business district, La Defense and the historical city centre.

A design competition in 1982 was won by Danish architect Johann Otto von Spreckelsen and engineer Erik Reitzel, who proposed a 20th century version of the Arc de Triomphe. La Grande Arche was opened in 1989 and immediately became a new French icon. The Arche is almost a hollow cube, measuring in excess of 100m in each dimension. Government offices are housed in the two sides and an exhibition centre in the roof section. The distinctive silhouette, combined with the now well established and expanding forest of other tall buildings of La Defense, acts as a brilliant beacon drawing visitors and business to this buzzing 21st century city sector.

Remarkably this planning strategy has provided a sustainable new commercial community, which will be able to expand further if needed, yet retain a strong connection to the city. La Defense complements but does not detract from, or impinge upon, the traditional character and appeal of Paris or its World Heritage status. In Scotland we sometimes seem frozen in awe of our heritage. It is truly amazing what can be done with a combination of political determination, far-sighted planning and innovative architecture and design.

Distinctive white domes at Sacre-Coeur Basilica, Paul Abadie (1914)

Gilded finials of Galeries Lafayette, Georges Chedanne and Ferdinand Chanut (1912),frame the distant view of Opera Garnier, Charles Garnier (1875)

Galerie Vivienne – an early and much emulated example of richly crafted retail arcade, Francois Jean Delannoy (1826)

The iconic Pompidou Centre by Piano and Rogers (1977) still draws a crowd in the sunshine

More easels than artists in chic Montmartre

THE LOUVRE PYRAMID

Cour Napoléon, Hector Lefuel (1857)

Louvre Pyramid, IM Pei (1989)

The elegant glass Pyramids provide an iconic image but also give light and shelter to the new spacious entrance hall below ground required to cope with the increasing volume of visitors to this spectacular gallery. RIAS Honorary Fellow Ian Ritchie's practice Rice Francis Ritchie (RFR) together with Nicolet Chartrand Knoll Ltd (Montreal) contributed to the engineering of the pyramids.

BASILICA OF SACRE COEUR

Paul Abadie (1875 - 1914)

The hill at Montmartre, featuring the Roman-Byzantine style, domed Sacre Coeur Basilica presents an unusual verticality in the city's rich skyline (viewed from the roof terrace cafe at Paris's stylish Galeries Lafayette).

Le Grande Arche, Johann Otto von Spreckelsen (1989), a gigantic monument to Humanity reflects the Arc de Triomphe

Metro Station, Hector Guimard (1900)

Haussmann's plan set mandatory rules for facades requiring the use of quarried stone, regular heights and floor levels giving an impression that the entire city comprises grand palaces, even where the sloping topography requires a stepped approach.

Arc de Triomphe, Jean Chalgrin (1806), dominates the Champs-Elysees

Distant view of Notre-Dame Catedrale (1345) reconstruction by Viollet-le-Duc (1870)

Distinctive windmill at the Moulin Rouge, Henri Mahé (1951)

PALAIS GARNIER

Charles Garnier (1875)

The exhuberant Paris Opera House was the result of a design competition held in 1861 and is probably one of the best known individual buildings to emerge from the comprehensive Haussmann reconstruction of Paris authorised by Emperor Napoleon III.

MONTMARTRE FUNICULAR

Francois Deslaugiers (1991)

A welcome alternative to climbing the long staircases at Rue Foyatier en route to Sacre Coeur. The original, water powered, funicular system of 1891 was rebuilt in 1935 and more recently has been redesigned with bright glassy stations at top and bottom and shining new trains.

EIFFEL TOWER

engineers: Maurice Koechlin & Emile Nouguier for Gustave Eiffel, architect: Stephen Sauvestre (1889)

It is now impossible to imagine Paris without this tower, yet the opposition to its construction was vociferous, involving many leading contemporary intellectuals, including Paris' best known architect Charles Garnier.

ROMA

41.90°N, 12.50°E

VIA DELLA LUNGARETTA, TRASTEVERE

Across the River Tiber the scale of buildings visibly reduces. Artisan workshops and narrow streets reinforce a bohemian atmosphere, giving a distinctive local character.

VISITORS ALMOST ALWAYS arrive in Rome with a huge list of 'must see' attractions. Flocks of walkers follow their flags, dragging heavy legs from fountain, to basilica, and on. It is unlikely that anything more than a slight understanding of the complex layers of this city can be gleaned this way, though, for some, that may be enough.

Rome is distinctive however in so many ways. You will never need to spend time editing road signs, barriers, yellow lines or traffic detritus, which so despoil your photographs of other beautiful cities. The 'Jeremy Clarkson school' of traffic management works remarkably well, passing huge volumes of indecently large cars, and clouds of Vespas quickly through often narrow, chaotic central streets. Free form haphazard parking is another latin art-form, which operates with surprisingly little aggravation, and sometimes even displays 'sprezzatura' – an Italian word that defines a certain nonchalance, which makes difficult tasks seem effortless.

Likewise, the dead hands of cost consultants seem totally absent over the 2,000+ years of construction and ongoing adaptation, which has created this Eternal City. Why build one stair where bi-parting risers could add symmetry? Huge floor to ceiling heights give gigantic, but beautifully proportioned, three or four storey palaces. Face to face they challenge each other across a Via clearly designed to allow only an Imperial Chariot and one horse to pass. Buildings for worship can, and do, go higher still. Casual exploration behind tall porticos is to be recommended. Everywhere in Rome, the visitor is rewarded with magnificent frescoes, sculptures, and design, each with provenance to match the world's best museums.

Every inch counts in Rome. No space lies unused, or under-used. Wherever your gaze falls there is tremendous evidence of human effort. Graffiti-ed shutters rise to reveal stunning, bright, high fashion display windows and stylish, expensive shops. Leather, glass, or furniture work-benches spill out from packed stockrooms, while bistros and cafes daily colonise those parts of the streets, which lesser cities reserve only for traffic wardens. 'Hole in the wall' retailing throughout the centre, gives an impression that Rome blossoms as the day emerges towards its highlight – 'passegiatta', that evening ritual where young Italians dress in style, and promenade to see and be seen.

The energetic bustle, which creates a busy market each weekday morning around the statue of Giordano Bruno in Campo dei Fiori, is matched by the efficient dismantling and barrowing back early each afternoon. This huge task eventually gives way to a ballet performed by rotating petite cleansing vehicles, who quickly remove bulk waste, scoosh water, and restore the piazza for more sophisticated al fresco evening uses.

The centre of Rome has few modern buildings. One notable exception however is the Ara Pacis Museum by Richard Meier. Evocative of his MACBA in Barcelona, Ara Pacis sits well on its prominent riverside site. The white travertine and glass gives a sparkling and airy Roman home for the rebuilt and restored Altar to Peace, dedicated to Augustus in 12BC.

While contemporary architects show exemplary innovative skills in reuse and adaptation of historic buildings, it can be engrossing also to explore the extent of previous layers of architectural interventions. The removal of gilded bronze roof tiles from the Pantheon in 663AD, and later reuse of further melted bronze ceilings from the porch, by Bernini in 1634, may appeal to green philosophy but it also seems a bit like vandalism. Part of the Baths of Diocletian (dating from 298AD), were also reconfigured to form a basilica, S.Maria degli Angeli, in 1563 by Michelangelo; further works created a transept in 1749 to a design by Vanvitelli, but still the mighty groin vaulting gives some idea of the appearance of the original Baths in antiquity. Across the road, Piazza Della Repubblica, was formed by extensive rebuilding, in 1887, of two semi-circular palaces, over the previous Esedra. The ancient walls and floors are again visible through glass floors installed in 2006 for the new Exedra Hotel, along with an innovative roof-top leisure pool.

The Eternal City cannot stand still, and mercifully thus far, refuses to become a 'theme park'. Innovative modern design compliments, enlivens and reinvigorates genuine world heritage sites and this too requires 'sprezzatura' – fortunately they've got it – in spades!

Crisp stylish retail appears when shutters rise

Ara Pacis –unique modern architecture in central Rome, designed by Richard Meier Architect (2006)

Ara Pacis, Richard Meier Architect (2006) – unusually modern architecture for central Rome

Exotic hole-in-wall shop trades behind graffiti covered shutters

The skyline of ancient Rome now bristles with modern roof terraces, restaurants and even swimming pools as at the Exedra Hotel (top left) and The Valadier Hotel (bottom left and right) which is named in honour of Giuseppe Valadier who designed the Piazza del Popolo in 1793

Tiny open air church yard packed with statuary for sale

Altar to Peace now beautifully accessible within Ara Pacis, Richard Meier Architect (2006)

PALAZZO DELLA CANCELLERIA

Attributed to Bramante (1513)

It is reported that this renaissance palace was built re-using travertine from nearby ruins, and that the granite columns were recycled from Rome's 'Theatre of Pompey'. Intelligent re-use is not new. Confiscated from a plotter found conspiring against the Medici family the Palazzo became and remains Vatican property.

SANTA MARIA IN TRASTEVERE

One of the oldest churches in Rome (c. 340AD). The facade features stunning mosaics and the piazza has become a popular meeting place.

THE PANTHEON

The best preserved Roman building (rebuilt c. 126AD) became a Christian church in the 7th century. The inscription on the pediment translates as "M(arcus) Agrippa, son of Lucius, made this building when consul for the third time". The gigantic granite Corinthian columns of the portico, each formed from a single piece of stone, were transported by boat from Egypt and floated down the Tiber to the site.

Columns from Theatro di Marcello

SANT'AGNESE IN AGONE
attributed to Francesco Borromini (1652)

The facade to Piazza Navona was so disliked by Bernini that his Four Rivers statues cower in terror of the anticipated collapse of Borromini's church.

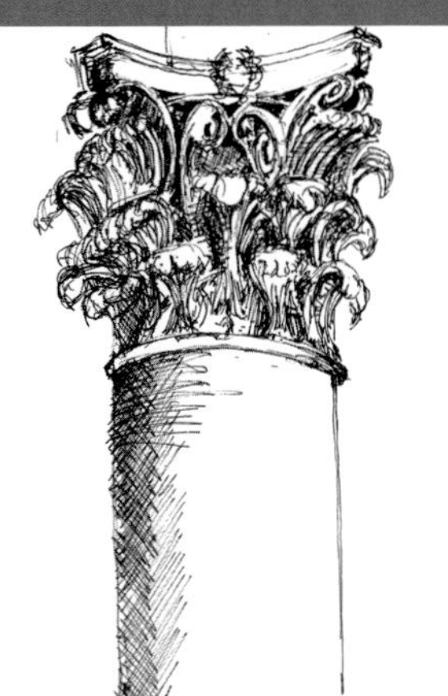

CAMPO DEL FIORE

ARA PACIS

Richard Meier Architect (2006)

Controversy still surrounds central Rome's most modern building. At one stage Mayor Gianni Alemanno campaigned to have the new building demolished, but the bright new architecture makes a comfortable and accessible home for the 2000 year old Altar to Peace originally dedicated to Augustus.

MAXXI

Zaha Hadid (2010)

An essay in sharp pointed irregular yet grand spaces this Stirling Prize winner is a decent walk from the ancient centre of Rome. It is a big building in what is predominantly a residential suburb but the gentle courtyard formed at the entrance will be a stunning location for sculpture or large installations.

ROME
Panoramic view across Rome from the top of Pincio at Viale del Belvedere.

PALAU DE LES ARTS REINA SOFIA

Santiago Calatrava (2005)

A cultural venue like no other, this opera house cantilevers from a tiny base, gains stability from soaring structural fins and merges sculpture and architecture.

VALÈNCIA 39.48°N, 0.37°W

FOUNDED IN 138BC, Valencia still has one of the most interesting historic centres in Spain. Medieval gates from the original city wall remain as at Torres de Serranos and early prosperity and commercial influence is evident in La Lonja de la Seda, "the Silk Exchange", dating from 1483. La Lonja's serene courtyard and "hall of columns" represent admirable Gothic secular architecture. The architect's name, Pere Compte, is too rarely mentioned.

Only very special architects become renowned and fewer still become eponymous with individual cities: John Wood's Bath; Gaudi's Barcelona; Mackintosh's Glasgow; Haussmann's Paris; acknowledge each architect's contribution. "Calatrava's Valencia" refers both to his birthplace and his inspiration in creating a unique, world class, destination within an already distinguished historical city.

Following severe flooding (1957) the River Turia was diverted around Valencia. The river bed quickly formed an unkempt but tranquil garden. In 1989 Joan Lerma, President of the Principality, championed a local Professor's idea to create a "city of arts and sciences" within this fertile but derelict river basin.

At a time when town planning was still the second degree of choice for most graduate architects, Santiago Calatrava preferred to follow his architectural studies with a course in engineering in Switzerland. This acknowledged his scientific interests but Calatrava is also a committed and capable architect-artist, painter and sculptor. His profound understanding of engineering, mathematics, sculpture and art has brought renown for creating uncompromisingly modern buildings.

Calatrava's sinuous communication tower at the Barcelona Olympics was applauded in 1992. In the same year he achieved acclaim in North America for the cathedral like 'Allen Lambert Galleria' in Toronto. International recognition made him an obvious choice as architect for Valencia's audacious regeneration project.

Working initially with Felix Candela on 'L'Oceanografic', a dynamic architectural contrast to historic Valencia became immediately obvious. Deep tanks and landscaped lakes, well suited to the dried out river bed, are topped by access pavilions with delicate hyperbolic paraboloid roofs. Like an iceberg most of the volume and interest here lies below the surface.

"Ciutat de les Arts i les Ciencies" was inaugurated with "L'Hemisferic" (1998). Glazed sides open like eyelids, revealing a spherical IMAX theatre. The white ribbed Science Museum provides bright exhibition halls and educational spaces on several levels. Cleverly concealed coach and car parking is contained beneath the elegant "Umbracle". The upper level of this soaring, open structure was designed for indigenous plants and sculptures – including one by Yoko Ono – as an attractive public entrance promenade. It now is a 'disco' venue - presumably generating significant income.

Throughout the vast site, shallow blue lagoons complement spectacular forms, giving photogenic viewpoints everywhere. An otherworldly appearance belies extremely refined design and circulation. Buildings and landscape effortlessly handle huge visitor volumes without stress. Grinning groups record themselves with camera phones held high – or low – against this surreal and totally exciting backdrop.

Intellectual justification for unpopular modernism is unnecessary here. This architecture – and even its architect – is popular and appreciated by all ages. Children see buildings with ears – and snouts. Teenagers enjoy space to rumble. Adults find serenity – even contemplation – amid a truly charismatic architecture.

TORRES DE SERRANOS

Pere Balaguer (1394)

These towers were never used for defense and remained after the city wall was removed in 1865 only because they were still in use as a prison.

LA LONJA

Pesto Compte; Juan Iborra, and Johan Corbera (1482-1533)

A trading hall designed to reinforce the power and wealth of merchants In the prosperous silk trade during the 15th and 16th centuries.

CAMPANAR DE LA CATEDRAL

Andreu Julia, followed by Joseph Franch and Pere Balaguer (1381)

The first view of the Cathedral for many visitors to Valencia will be the wide octagonal bell tower with the flat top which looks onto busy Placa de la Reina.

L'Umbracle with concealed parking decks behind the nose of L'Hemispheric, Calatrava (1998)

Approach to Santiago Calatrava's 'City within the city'

Orange trees grow freely in diverted river bed, Valencia

Bright Spanish crockery

Santiago Calatrava's huge exposed skeleton structure at the Museum of Science (1998)

Felix Candella's aquarium below ground at the City of Science (1998)

Plaza de la Virgen, Valencia Cathedral

Modern pavilion to protect Valencia's Roman remains.

EL MUSEUM DE LES CIENCIES PRINCIPE FELIPE

Santiago Calatrava (1999)

The end elevation of this science museum gives no indication of the elegant concrete skeleton which supports all three main levels and is exposed along the building's full length.

L'HEMISPHERIC

Santiago Calatrava (1998)

The inaugural building in this city within a city was the planetarium with sides which can open like eyelids and an IMAX theatre, like the pupil at the centre.

EL CONQUISTADOR

'Spanish School' bronze statue (1890)

The equestrian statue of Jaime I, set amid an eclectic range of buildings at Parc Parterre, celebrates this liberator of Valencia from rule by the Moors.

IAN STUART CAMPBELL CiB, MSAI, Hon FRIAS

Edinburgh based, Ian Stuart Campbell studied at the Mackintosh School of Architecture. He is an enthusiastic artist and designer who considers drawing, painting and photography to be essential tools in any design process.

Stuart has special interest in urban design, conceptual planning and design communication and has practical experience in the design of major commercial projects as a Director with Hugh Martin Partnership (subsequently Archial Architects) based in Edinburgh. "It seems to me that the opportunity to take time to look, and look again, at buildings, patterns of life, and dynamics of space in fabulous places such as Rome, Paris or Edinburgh is a real privilege." observes Stuart, "Especially so when the solitary act of rough sketching becomes a social encounter or the drawing is enjoyed, admired or even (on occasions) purchased by others."

This rough sketching project found its origins during a Hugh Martin Partnership practice visit to Barcelona in late 2007. Once the camera had failed to fully capture the overwhelming magic of that astonishing place, drawing seemed like the only alternative.

Stuart's ongoing project involves interpreting successful architecture and public spaces in cities throughout Europe and Scandinavia. Rough sketching is usually carried out on site where the ink marks are committed directly to paper without any pre-drafting in pencil or any technical set up. Stuart's original sketches are drawn using Staedler pigment ink pens, which are chosen for lightfast and waterproof qualities and ease of use in the open air. Whenever possible sketches are drawn on Fabriano 220/300 gsm smooth paper, or equivalent.

MEMBERSHIPS

Honorary Fellow of the Royal Incorporation of Architects in Scotland (Hon FRIAS); Honorary Secretary and Exhibiting member, the Scottish Society of Architect Artists (SSAA); Member Society of Architectural and Industrial Illustrators (MSAI); Member of British Association of Industrial Editors (BAIE); Member of British Association of Communicators in Business (CiB); Member of The Society of Scottish Artists; Associate Member of Performing Rights Society (PRS) (category: writer and arranger); Contributor to architectural and design publications including *RIAS Prospect*, *Building*, *Building Design*, *Property Executive*, the *RIBA Journal* and *RIAS Quarterly*.

SHARON McCORD Hon FRIAS

26.2.1967 – 11.11.2012

Sharon McCord was born in Fauldhouse, West Lothian. She studied English at Glasgow University where she wrote for, and edited the student newspaper, the Guardian. For over a decade after University she worked as a journalist under the 'nom de guerre', Sara Villiers. Although she later airily dismissed 'Sara's' regular, girl about town, columns as "breathless, hedonistic, piffle" her huge volume and sheer quality of work as a features writer and critic for, among others, the Herald, Scotsman, Scotland on Sunday, Guardian and Telegraph led to recognition in the Young Journalist of the Year Awards. Beautiful, stylish, raven-haired and adorned with bright red lipstick, she personified the 'it girl' before anyone invented the term, although, typically witty and self-deprecating, her own description had her as "the Carrie Bradshaw of Sauchiehall Street"!

From the early 2000s Sharon reverted to her own name and pursued a career in events management and communications for membership organisations, ultimately, from 2007, for the Royal Incorporation of Architects in Scotland (RIAS) where, she declared, she had, at last, found her vocation. As Depute Secretary, she reinvented the RIAS journal, significantly increased the organisation's public and political profile, overhauled its communications, introduced ebulletins, set up a new website and organised numerous distinctive and successful events. Much of this was done after the diagnosis of terminal kidney cancer in 2009. Her brave blog www.kidneycancerinfo.org.uk, has, with typical humour and candour, supported and informed many of those suffering from the condition.

Supported by her beloved husband Robin McKechnie, Sharon spent her last ten days in the St Columba's Hospice, Edinburgh and died on Remembrance Day 2012. She is survived by Robin, her parents Patsy and Jimmy, sisters Jackey and Louise and brother Jason.

SHARON McCORD Hon FRIAS

26.2.1967 – 11.11.2012

Sharon's knowledge and experience of journalism gave her a very clear vision of a new member's magazine for the Royal Incorporation of Architects In Scotland. Infectious enthusiasm and innovative thinking ensured that her proposed format for the new *RIAS Quarterly* was readily adopted, enjoyed by readers and still remains the inspiration for that publication.

After viewing an exhibition in Rutland Square by the Scottish Society of Architect Artists, (SSAA) Sharon was generous enough to suggest that my ink sketches could be included in the forthcoming (second) issue of 'Quarterly' ... on the condition that I could also write a short piece to accompany them ... and, oh yes, did I also have some photographs? Thus the format for the regular sketch features in *RIAS Quarterly* was born.

Sharon's clever structure for these short articles proved ideal for my burgeoning 'Grand Tour' of European cities. Interest in what makes distinctive places so alluring rekindled my enthusiasm for 'rough sketching'. Drawing on location as a memory aid has the advantage that the senses get time to comfortably absorb atmosphere, activity, smells and sounds. The addional discipline of making notes extends this experience in areas where sketching may be limited and hopefully rounds first impressions into a more valuable memory.

I am immensely grateful to Sharon for the encouragement which helped turn a hobby into an engrossing study. It is entirely appropriate therefore that this publication should be dedicated to the memory of Sharon McCord, Hon FRIAS.

Stuart Campbell

ST COLUMBA'S HOSPICE

MISSION:

"St Columba's Hospice aims to improve the lives of people in Edinburgh and the Lothian's with life limiting disease. We provide the highest standard of palliative care and offer emotional, spiritual and practical support for our patients, their families and loved ones. Every year we care for over 1000 patients, and as a charity we rely on the support of our local community to ensure that we can continue this vital work."

www.stcolumbashospice.org.uk